How to Start a Manufacturing Business

A Step by Step Guide to Starting a New Small Manufacturing Company

MEIR LIRAZ

Published by BizMove
www.bizmove.com

Table of Contents

MEIR LIRAZ

1. Things to Consider Before You Start

This guide will walk you step by step through all the essential phases of starting a successful manufacturing business. To profit in a manufacturing based business, you need to consider the following questions: What business am I in? What goods do I sell? Where is my market? Who will buy? Who is my competition? What is my sales strategy? What merchandising methods will I use? How much money is needed to operate my company? How will I get the work done? What management controls are needed? How can they be carried out?

No one can answer such questions for you. As the owner-manager you have to answer them and draw up your business plan. The pages of this Guide are a combination of text and workspaces so you can write in the information you gather in developing your business plan - a logical progression from a commonsense starting point to a commonsense ending point.

It takes time and energy and patience to draw up a satisfactory business plan. Use this Guide to get your ideas and the supporting facts down on paper. And, above all, make changes in your plan on these pages as that plan unfolds and you see the need for changes.

Bear in mind that anything you leave out of the picture will create an additional cost, or drain on your money, when it unexpectedly crops up later on. If you leave out or ignore enough items, your business is headed for disaster.

Keep in mind, too, that your final goal is to put your plan into action. More will be said about this step near the end of this Guide.

What's in This for Me?

Time was when an individual could start a business and prosper provided you were strong enough to work long hours and had the knack for selling for more than the raw materials or product cost. Small store, grist mills, livery stables, and blacksmith shops sprang up in many crossroad communities as Americans applied their energy and native intelligence to settling the continent.

Today this native intelligence is still important. But by itself the common sense for which Americans are famous will not insure success in a business. Technology, the marketplace, and even people themselves have become more complicated than they were 100, or even 25, years ago.

Common sense must be combined with new techniques in order to succeed in the space age. Just as one would not think of launching a manned space capsule without a flight plan, so one should not think of launching a new manufacturing business without a business plan.

A business plan is an exciting tool that you can use to plot a "course" for your company. Such a plan is a logical progression from a commonsense starting point to a commonsense ending point.

To build a business plan for your company, an owner-manager needs only to think and react as a manager to questions such as: What product is to be manufactured?

How can it best be made? What will it cost me? Who will buy the product? What profit can I make?

Why Am I in Business

If you're like most business people, you're in business to make money and be your own boss. But, few business people would be able to say that those are the only reasons. The money that you will make from your business will seldom seem like enough for all the long hours, hard work, and responsibility that go along with being the boss.

Then, why do so many stay in business?

This is hardly the time for philosophy. If you're starting or expanding a business, you have enough to think about. But, whether or not you even think about it, the way you operate your business will reflect your "business philosophy."

Consider this. An owner-manager inspects a production run and finds a minor defect. Even though in nine out of ten cases the user of the product would not notice the defect, the owner decides to scrap the entire run.

What does this tell you? It shows that he (or she) gets an important reward from doing what is the right thing - in this case, providing a quality product.

The purpose of this section is not to play down the importance of making a profit. Profits are important. They will keep your business going and attract additional capital into your business. But you should be aware that there are other rewards and responsibilities associated with having your own business.

In your planning, you might give some thought to your responsibilities to employees, community, stockholders, customers, product, and profit. Jot these down. Later when you've lined-up your management team, discuss this subject with them. This type of group thinking will help everyone, including yourself, understand the basic purposes for each day's work.

Even though you won't advertise it throughout your market, the way you operate your business will reflect your business philosophy.

What Business Am I in?

In making your business plan, the next question to consider is: What business an I really in? At first reading, this question may seem silly. "If there is one thing I know," you say to yourself, "it is what business I'm in." But hold on. Some owner-managers go broke and others waste their savings because they are confused about the business they are really in.

The experience of an old line manufacturing company provides an example of dealing with the question: What business am I really in? In the early years of this century, the founder of the company had no trouble answering the question. As he put it, "I make and sell metal trash cans." This answer held true for his son until the mid-1950's when sales began to drop off. After much thought, the son decided he was in the container business.

Based on this answer, the company dropped several of its lines of metal trash cans, modified other lines, and introduced new products, such as shipping cartons used by other manufacturers and Government agencies.

What business am I in? (Write your answer here)

_____

Asking questions like: What does my product do for my customer? Why? Where? How? What doesn't it do? What should it do later but doesn't do now? can lead to the ultimate conclusion of what business you're in and possibly direct you to new lines of products or enterprises.

2. How to Plan Your Marketing

When you have decided what business you're really in, you have just made your first marketing decision. Now you must face other marketing consideration.

Successful marketing starts with you, the owner-manager. You have to know your product, your market, your customers, and your competition.

Before you plan production, you have to decide who your market is, where it is, why they will buy your product, whether it is a growth or static market, if there are any seasonal aspects of the market, and what percentage of the market you will shoot for in the first, second, and third year of operation. Your production goals and plans must be based on and be responsive to this kind of fact finding (market feasibility and research).

The narrative and work blocks that follow are designed to help you work out a marketing plan. Your objective is to determine what needs to be done to bring in sales dollars.

In some directories, marketing information is listed according to the Standard Industrial Classification (SIC) of the product and industry. The SIC classifies firms by the type of activity they're engaged in, and it is used to promote the uniformity and comparability of statistical data relating to market research. When you begin your market research, you may find it useful to have alread / lassified your products according to this code. (The Standard Industrial Classification Manual may be available at your library.)

Product / Sic No.

1. _____ / _____

2. _____ / _____

Market Area

Where and to whom are you going to sell your product? Describe the market area you will serve in terms of geography and customer profile:

_____

Who Are Your Competitors?

List your principal competitors selling in your market area, estimate their percentage of market penetration and dollar sales in that market, and estimate their potential loss of sales as a result of your entry into the market.

Name of Competitor and Location	% Share of Market	Estimated Sales	Sales Loss Because of You
1. _____	_____	_____	_____
2. _____	_____	_____	_____
3. _____	_____	_____	_____
4. _____	_____	_____	_____

How Do You Rate Your Competition?

Try to find out the strengths and weaknesses of each competitor. Then write your opinion of each of your principal competitors, their principal products, facilities, marketing characteristics, and new product development or adaptability to changing market conditions.

_____

Have any of your competitors recently closed operations or have they withdrawn from your market area? (State reasons if you know them):

———————

Advantages Over Competitors

On what basis will you be able to capture your projected share of the market? Below is a list of characteristics which may indicate the advantages your product(s) enjoy over those offered by competitors. Indicate those advantages by placing a check in the proper space. If there is more than one competitor, you may want to make more than one checklist. Attach these to the worksheet.

Analyze each characteristic. For example, a higher price may not be a disadvantage if the product is of higher quality than your competitor's. You may want to make a wish to spell out the specifics of each characteristic and explain where your product is disadvantaged and how this will be overcome, attach it to this worksheet. Also, the unique characteristics of your product can be the basis for advertising and sales promotion.

Remember, the more extensive your planning, the more your business plan will help you.

Product(s)	Product No. 1	Product No. 2
Price	_____	_____
Performance	_____	_____
Durability	_____	_____
Versatility	_____	_____
Speed or accuracy	_____	_____
Ease of operation or use	_____	_____
Ease of maintenance or repair	_____	_____
Ease or cost of installation	_____	_____
Size or weight	_____	_____
Styling or appearance	_____	_____
Other characteristics not listed:		
_____	_____	_____
_____	_____	_____

What, if anything, is unique about your product?

_____

Distribution

How will you get your product to the ultimate consumer?
Will you sell it directly through your own sales organization
or indirectly through manufacturer's agents, brokers,
wholesalers, and so on. (Use the blank to write a brief
statement of your method of distribution and manner of
sales):

_____

What will this method of distribution cost you?

_____

Do you plan to use special marketing, sales or
merchandising techniques? Describe them here:

———————

List your customers by name, the total amount they buy from you, and the amount they spend for each of your products.

———————

Market Trends

What has been the sales trend in your market area for your principal product(s) over the last 5 years? What do you expect it to be 5 years from now? You should indicate the source of your data and the basis of your projections. (This is a marketing research problem. It will require you to do some digging in order to come up with a market projection. Trade Associations will probably be your most helpful source of information. The Bureau of Census publishes a great deal of useful statistics). Industry and product statistics are usually indicated in dollars, Units, such as numbers of customers, numbers of items sold, etc., may be used, but also relate your sales to dollars.

———————

List the name and address of trade associations which serve your industry and indicate whether or not you are a member.

_____ the name and address of other organizations, governmental agencies, industry and indicate whether or not you are a member.

———————

Share of the Market

What percentage of total sales in your market area do you expect to obtain for your products after your facility is in full operation?

Sales Volume

What sales volume do you expect to reach with your products?

Production

Production is the work that goes on in a factory that results in a product. In making your business plan, you have to consider all the activities that are involved in turning raw materials into finished products. The work blocks which follow are designed to help you determine what production facilities and equipment you need.

Manufacturing Operation

List the basic operations for example, cut and sew, machine and assemble, etc., which are needed in order to make your product.

_____

Raw Materials

What raw materials or components will you need, and where will you get them?

What amount of raw material and/or components will you need to stock?

_____

Are there any special considerations concerning the storage requirements of your raw material? For example, will you use chemicals which can only be stored for a short time before they lose their potency?

_____

Equipment

List the equipment needed to perform the manufacturing operations. Indicate whether you will rent or buy the equipment and the cost to you.

Your equipment facilities, and method of operation must comply with the Occupational Safety and Health Act. You may obtain a copy of Standards for General Industry from a field office of the Occupational Safety and Health Administration.

Labor Skills

List the labor skills needed to run the equipment:

_____

List the indirect labor, for example: material handlers, stockmen, janitors, and so on, that is needed to keep the plant operating:

_____

If persons with these skills are not already on your payroll, where will you get them?

_____

Space

How much space will you need to make the product? Include restrooms, storage for raw material and for finished products, and employee parking facilities if appropriate. Are there any local ordinances you must comply with?

_____

_____

Do you own this space? Yes _____ No _____

Will you buy this space? Yes _____ No _____

Will you lease this space? Yes _____ No _____

How much will it cost you? Yes _____ No _____

Overhead

List the overhead items which will be needed in addition to indirect labor and include their cost. Examples are: tools, supplies, utilities, office help, telephone, payroll taxes, holidays, vacations, and salaries for your key people (sales manager, plant manager, and foreman).

3. How Much Money Will You Need?

Money is a tool you can use to make your plan work. Money is also a measuring device. You will measure your plan in terms of dollars; and outsiders, such as bankers and other lenders, will do the same.

When you determine how much money is needed to start (or expand) your business, you can decide whether or not to move ahead. If the cost is greater than the profits which the business can make, there are two things to consider. Many businesses do not show a profit until the second or third year of operation. If this looks like the case with your business, you will need the plans and financial reserves to carry you through this period. On the other hand, maybe you would be better off putting your money into stocks, bonds or other reliable investments rather than taking on the time consuming job of managing a business.

Like most businesses, your new business or expansion will require a loan. The burden of proof in borrowing money is upon the borrower. You have to show the banker or other lender how the borrowed money will be spent. Even more important, the lender needs to know how and when you will repay the loan.

To determine whether or not your plan is economically feasible, you need to pull together three sets of figures:

(1) Expected sales and expense figures for 12 months.

(2) Cash flow figures for 12 months.

(3) Current balance sheet figures.

Than visit your banker. Remember, your banker or lender is your friend not your enemy. So, meet regularly. Share all the information and data you possess. If the lender is ready to help, he (or she) needs to know not only your strengths but also your weaknesses.

Expected Sales and Expenses Figures

To determine whether or not your business can make its way in the market place, you should estimate your sales and expenses for 12 months.

Projected Statement of Sales and Expenses for One Year

	Jan	Feb	Mar	Apr	May	Jun	Jul	Aug	Sep	Oct	Nov	Dec	Total
A. Net Sales													
B. Cost of Goods Sold													
1. Raw Materials													
2. Direct Labor													
3. Manufacturing Overhead													
Indirect Labor													
Factory Heat & Power													
Insurance and Taxes													
Depreciation													
C. Gross Margin (Subtract B from A)													
D. Selling and Administrative Expenses													
4. Salaries and Commissions													
5. Advertising Expenses													
6. Miscellaneous Expenses													
E. Net Operating Profit (Subtract D from C)													
F. Interest Expense													
G. Net Profit before Taxes (Subtract F from E)													
H. Estimated Income Tax													
I. Net Profit after Income Tax (Subtract H from G)													

Cash Flow Figures

Estimates of future sales will not pay an owner-manager's bills. Cash must flow into the business at the proper times if bills are to be paid and a profit realized at the end of the year. To determine whether your projected sales and expense figures are realistic, you should prepare a cash flow forecast for the 12 months covered by your estimates of sales and expenses.

Estimated Cash Forecast

	Jan	Feb	Mar	Apr	May	Jun	Jul	Aug	Sep	Oct	Nov	Dec
(1) Cash in Bank (Start of Month)												
(2) Petty Cash (Start of Month)												
(3) Total Cash (add (1) and (2)												
(4) Expected Accounts Receivable												
(5) Other Money Expected												
(6) Total Receipts (add (4) and (5))												
(7) Total Cash and Receipts (add (3) and (6)												
(8) All Disbursements (for month)												
(9) Cash Balance at end of Month in Bank Account and Petty Cash (subtract (8) from (7)*												

*This balance is your starting figure for the next month

Current Balance Sheet Figures

A balance sheet shows the financial conditions of a business as of a certain date. It lists what a business has, what it owes, and the investment of the owner. A balance sheet enable you to see at a glance your assets and liabilities.

Getting the Work Done

Your manufacturing business is only part way home when you have planned your marketing and production. Organization is needed if your plant is to produce what you expect it to produce.

Organization is essential because you as the owner-manager probably cannot do all the work.

You'll have to delegate work, responsibility, and authority. A helpful tool in getting this done is the organization chart. It shows at a glance who is responsible for the major activities of a business. However, no matter how your operation is organized, keep control of the financial management.

In the beginning, the president of the small manufacturing company probably does everything.

It is important that you recognize your weaknesses early in the game and plan to get assistance wherever you need it. This may be done using consultants on an as-needed basis, by hiring the needed personnel, or by retaining a lawyer and accountant.

The workblock below lists some of the areas you may want to consider. Adapt it to your needs and indicate who will take care of the various functions. (one name may appear more than once.)

Manufacturing _____

Marketing _____

Research and Technical Backup

_____

Accounting _____

Legal _____

Insurance _____

Other:

_____

_____

_____

Making Your Plan Work

To make your plan work you will need feedback. For example, the year end profit and loss (income) statement shows whether your business made a profit or loss for the past 12 months.

But you can't wait 12 months for the score. To keep your plan on target you need readings at frequent intervals. A profit and loss statement at the end of each month or at the end of each quarter is one type of frequent feedback. However, the P and L may be more of a loss than a profit statement if you rely only on it. In addition, your cash flow projection must be continuously updated and revised as necessary. You must set up management controls which will help you insure that the right things are being done from day to day and from week to week.

The management control system which you set up should give you precise information on: inventory, production, quality, sales, collection of accounts receivable, and disbursement. The simpler the system, the better. Its purpose is to give you and your key people current information in time to correct deviations from approved policies, procedures, or practices. You are after facts with emphasis on trouble spots.

Inventory Control

The purpose of controlling inventory is to provide maximum service to your customers. Your aim should be to achieve a rapid turnover on your inventory, the fewer dollars you tie up in raw materials inventory and in finished goods inventory, the better. Or, saying it in reverse, the faster you get back your investment in raw materials and finished goods inventory, the faster you can reinvest your capital to meet additional consumer needs.

In setting up inventory controls, keep in mind that the cost of the inventory is not your only cost. There are inventory costs, such as the cost of purchasing, the cost of keeping inventory records, and the cost of receiving and storing raw materials.

Production

In preparing this business plan, you have estimated the cost figures for your manufacturing operation. Use these figures as the basis for standards against which you can measure your day-to-day operations to make sure that the clock does not nibble away at profits. These standards will help you to keep machine time, labor man-hours, process time, delay time, and down time within your projected cost figures. Periodic production reports will allow you to keep your finger on potential drains on your profits and should also provide feedback on your overhead expense.

Quality Control

Poorly made products cause a company to lose customers. In addition, when a product fails to perform satisfactorily, shipments are held up, inventory is increased, and a severe financial strain can result. Moreover, when quality is poor, it's a good bet that waste and spoilage on the production line are greater than they should be. The details - checkpoints, reports and so on - of your quality control system will depend on your type of production system. In working out these details, keep in mind that their purpose is to answer one question: What needs to be done to see that the work is right the first time? Will you have to do extensive quality control on raw materials? This is an added expense you must consider.

Sales

To keep on top of sales, you will need answers to questions, such as: How many sales were made? What was the dollar amount? What products were sold? At what price? What delivery dates were promised? What credit terms were given to customers?

It is also important that you set up an effective collection system for "accounts receivable," so that you don't tie up your capital in aging accounts.

Disbursement

Your management controls should also give you information about the dollars your company pays out. In checking on your bills, you do not want to be penny-wise and pound-foolish. You need to know that major items, such as paying bills on time get the supplier's discount, are being handled according to your policies. Your review system should also give you the opportunity to make judgments on the use of funds. In this manner, you can be on top of emergencies as well as routine situations. Your system should also keep you aware that tax moneys, such as payroll income tax deductions, are set aside and paid out at the proper time.

4. Break-Even Analysis

Break-even analysis is a management control device because the break-even point shows about how much you must sell under given conditions in order to just cover your costs with No profit and No loss.

In preparing to start or expand a manufacturing business you should determine at what approximate level of sales a new product will pay for itself and begin to bring in a profit.

Profit depends on sales volume, selling price, and costs. So, to figure your break-even point, first separate your fixed costs, such as rent or depreciation allowance, from your variable costs per unit, such as direct labor and materials.

The formula is:

break-even volume =

$$\frac{\text{total fixed costs}}{\text{selling price - variable cost per unit}}$$

For example, Ajax Plastics has determined its fixed costs to be $100,000 and variable costs to be $50 per unit. If the selling price per unit is $100, then Ajax's break-even volume is break-even volume =

$100,000

$$\frac{\$100,000}{\$100 - \$50} = 2000 \text{ units}$$

Earlier you estimated your expected sales for each product and total sales. Compute the break-even point for each.

Product 1: _____ Product 2: _____ Total Sales: _____

Keeping Your Plan Up to Date

The best made business plan gets out of date because conditions change. Sometimes the change is within your company, for example, several of your skilled operators quit their jobs. Sometimes the change is with customers. Their desires and tastes shift. For example, a new idea can sweep the county in 6 months and die overnight. Sometimes the change is technological as when new raw materials and components are put on the market.

In order to adjust a business plan to account for such changes, an owner-manager must:

(1) Be alert to the changes that come about in your company, in your industry, in your market, and in your community.

(2) Check your plan against these changes.

(3) Determine what revisions, if any, are needed in your plan.

You may be able to delegate parts of this work. For example, you might assign your shop foreman the task of watching for technical changes as reported in trade journals for your industry. Or you might expect your sales manager to keep you abreast of significant changes that occur in your markets.

But you cannot delegate the hardest part of this work. You cannot delegate the decisions as to what revision will be made in your plan. As owner-manager you have to make those judgments on an on-going basis.

When judgments are wrong, cut your losses as soon as possible and learn from the experience. The mental anguish caused by wrong judgments is part of the price you pay for being your own boss. You get your rewards from the satisfaction and profits that result from correct judgments.

Sometimes, serious problems can be anticipated and a course of action planned. For example, what if sales are 25 percent lower than you anticipated, or costs are 10 percent higher? You have prepared what you consider a reasonable budget. It might be a good idea to prepare a "problem budget," based on either lower sales, higher costs, or a combination of the two.

You will also have to exercise caution if your sales are higher than you anticipated. The growth in sales may only be temporary. Plan your expansion. New equipment and additional personnel could prove to be crippling if sales return to a previous lower level.

Keep in mind that few owner-managers are right 100 percent of the time. They can improve their batting average by operating with a business plan and by keeping that plan up to date.

5. How to Set Optimal Prices

In setting prices in a Manufacturing Firm, the goal should be to maximize profit. Although some owner-managers feel that an increased sales volume is needed for increased profits, volume alone does not mean more profit. The ingredients of profit are costs, selling price, and the unit sales volume. They must be in the proper proportions if the desired profit is to be obtained.

No one st prices formula will produce the greatest profit under all conditions. To price for maximum profit, the owner-manager must understand the different types of costs and how they behave. You need the up-to-date knowledge of market conditions because the "right" selling price for a product under one set of market conditions may be the wrong price at another time.

The "best" price for a product is not necessarily the price that will sell the most units. Nor is it always the price that will bring in the greatest number of sales dollars. Rather the "best" price is one that will maximize the profits of the company.

The "best" selling price should be cost orientated and market orientated. It should be high enough to cover your costs and help you make a profit. It should also be low enough to attract customers and build sales volume.

Set Prices - A Four Layer Cake

In determining the best selling price, think of price as being like a four layer cake. The four elements in your price are:

(1) the direct costs,

(2) manufacturing overhead,

(3) non-manufacturing overhead, and

(4) profit.

Direct costs are fairly easy to keep in mind. They are the cost of the material and the direct labor required to make a new product. You have these costs for the new product only when you make it.

On the other hand, even if you don't make the new product, you have manufacturing overhead such as janitor service, depreciation of machinery, and building repairs, which must be charged to old products. Similarly, non-manufacturing overhead such as selling and administrative expenses (including your salary) must be charged to your old products.

Direct Costing

The direct costing approach to setting prices enables you to start with known figures when you determine a price for a new product. For example, suppose that you are considering a price for a new product whose direct costs - materials and direct labor - are $3. Suppose further that you set the price at $5. The difference ($5 minus $3 = $2) is "contribution." For each unit sold, $2 will be available to help absorb your manufacturing overhead and your non-manufacturing overhead and to contribute toward profit.

Price-Volume Relationship

Any price above $3 will make some contribution toward your overhead costs which are already there whether or not you bring the product to market. The amount of contribution will depend on the selling price which you select and on the number of units that you sell at that price. Look for a few moments at some figures which illustrate this price-volume-contribution relationship:

Selling Price	$5	$4	$12
Projected sales in units	10,000	30,000	5,000
Projected dollar sales	$50,000	$120,000	$60,000
Direct costs ($3 per unit)	$30,000	$90,000	$45,000
Contribution	$20,000	$30,000	$15,000

In this example, the $4 selling price, assuming that you can sell 30,000 units, would be the "best price" for your product. However, if you could sell only 15,000 units at $4, the best price would be $5. The $5 selling price would bring in a $20,000 contribution against the $15,000 contribution from 15,000 units at $4.

With these facts in mind, you can use a market-orientated approach to set your selling price. Your aim is to determine the combination of selling price and unit volume which will provide the greater contribution toward your manufacturing overhead, non-manufacturing overhead, and profit.

Setting Prices Complications

If you ran a non-manufacturing company and could get as much of a product as you could sell, using the direct costing technique to determine your selling price would be fairly easy. Your success would depend on how well you could project unit sales volume at varying selling prices.

However, in a manufacturing company, various factors complicate the setting of a price. Usually, the quantity of a product that you can manufacture in a given time is limited. Also whether you ship directly to customers or manufacture for inventory has a bearing on your production and financial operation. Sometimes your production may be limited by labor. Sometimes by the availability of raw materials. And sometimes by practices of your competition. You have to recognize such factors in order to maximize your profits.

The direct costing concept enables you to key your pricing formula to that particular resource - labor, equipment, or material - which is in the shortest supply. The Gail Manufacturing Company provides an example.

Establish Contribution Percentage

In order to use the direct costing approach, Mr. Gail had to establish a contribution percentage. He set it at 40 percent. From past records, he determined that, over a 12-month period, a 40-percent contribution for each price would take care of manufacturing overhead and profit. In arriving at this figure, Mr. Gail considered sales volume as well as overhead costs.

Determining the contribution percentage is a vital step in using the direct costing approach to pricing. You should review your contribution percentage periodically to be sure that it covers all your overhead (including interest on money you may have borrowed for new machines or for building an inventory of finished products) and to be sure it provides for profit.

Mr. Gails' 40-percent contribution meant that direct costs - material and indirect labor - would be 60 percent of the selling price (100-40=60). Here is an example of how Mr. Gail computed his minimum selling price:

Material   27c
Direct labor +10c
_____
     37c

The 37 cents was 60 percent of the selling price which worked out to 62 cents (37 cents divided by 60 percent). The contribution was 25 cents (40 percent of selling price):

Selling price   62c
Direct costs   -37c
_____
    25c

In this approach, raw material is given the same importance as direct labor in determining the selling price.

Value of Material

The value of the material used in manufacturing the product has a bearing on the contribution dollars that will accrue from each unit sold. Suppose, in the example above, that the material costs are only 15 cents instead of 27 cents while the direct labor costs remain the same - 10 cents. Total direct costs would be 25 cents.

In order to get a maximum contribution of 40 percent - as Mr. Gail did - the direct costs must not exceed 60 percent of the selling price. To arrive at the selling price, divide the total direct cost by 60 percent (25 cents divided by .60). The selling price is 42 cents. With this new selling price, the contribution is 17 cents (42 cents minus 25 cents for direct costs.)

The point to remember is that when the material costs are less, the contribution will be less. This is true even though the same amount of direct labor and the same amount of machine use is required to convert the raw material into the finished product.

Contribution Per Labor Hour

What happens if Mr. Gail is unable to operate the equipment fully at all time? In order to maximize profits, he must realize the same dollar contribution per direct labor dollar, regardless of the cost materials. To do this, Mr. Gail could use the "Contribution per Labor Hour" Formula for setting his selling prices.

In this formula, you determine a mark-on percentage to use on your direct labor costs. This mark-on will provide the required contribution as percentage of selling price. For example, if direct labor is 10 cents and contribution is 25 cents, then contribution as a percentage of direct labor will be:

$$\frac{25}{10} = 250\%$$

The mark-on factor to use on direct labor costs is 250 percent of direct labor costs.

Now suppose that material is 15 cents and direct labor cost is 10 cents. The selling price would be 50 cents, figured as follows:

Material costs	15c
Direct labor	+10c
	——
	25c
Contribution	+25c
	——
Selling Price	= 50c

The "Contribution per Labor Hour" approach assures Mr. Gail a 25 cent contribution for each 10 cents of labor (250 percent) used to make a product regardless of the value of the raw material used.

Contribution-Per-Pound

If, and when, raw materials are in short supply and are the limiting factor, then the base to use is the dollar contribution-per-pound of material. This formula is similar to the one for contribution per labor hour. The difference is that you establish the contribution as a percentage of material cost rather than as a percentage of direct labor cost.

Contribution-Per-Machine-Hour

Determining the contribution-per-machine-hour can be a more involved task than figuring the contribution-per-pound. If different products are made on the same machine, each may use a different amount of machine time. This fact means that the total output of a certain machine in a given time period may vary. As a consequence, the dollar contribution-per-machine-hour that a company realizes may vary from product to product. For example, products A, B, and C are made on the same machine and their contribution-per-machine-hour is:

$28.80 for product A

$26.00 for product B

$20.00 for product C.

When machine capacity is the limiting factor, you can maximize profit by using dollar contribution-per-machine-hour when setting prices. When selling to customers, you should give priority to products that give the greatest dollar contribution-per-machine-hour. In the above example, your sales rep would push product A over products B and C.

To use this pricing approach means that you have to establish a base dollar contribution-per-machine-hour for each machine group. You do it by determining the total number of machine hours available in a given time period. You then relate these machine hours to the manufacturing and non-manufacturing overhead to be absorbed in that period. For example:

Total machine hours available in 12 months = 5,000

Total manufacturing and non-manufacturing overhead = $100,000

Contribution required per machine hour to cover manufacturing

and non-manufacturing overhead = $20*

* $100,000 divided by 5,000 hours

In this example, during periods when the company can sell output of all of its available machine hours, it must realize a return of $20 per machine hour in order to cover its manufacturing and non-manufacturing overhead. When the full 5,000 hours are used, the $20 per-hour return will bring the company to its break even point. When all the company's available machine hours cannot be sold, its return per-machine-hour must be more than $20.

Notice that in the above example, only the break even point is considered. There is no provision for profit. How do you build profit into this pricing formula?

Return-on-investments is a good approach. If the Gail Manufacturing Company, for example, has $300,000 invested and wants a 10 percent return, its profit before taxes would have to be $30,000. Mr. Gail can relate this profit goal to the machine-hour approach by dividing the $30,000 by 5,000 (the available machine hours). This means that he needs $6 per machine hour as a mark-up for profit.

Selling Price For Product C

now suppose that Mr. Gail wants to use the contribution-per-machine-hour and profit-per-machine hour approach to set a price for product C. For product C, the direct labor cost per unit is $1.80. Machine output (or units per hour) is 1.25, required contribution per machine hour is $20, and desired profit per machine hour is $6. The formula to set the unit selling price is:

Material cost	21.37
Direct labor	1.80
Contribution per Unit	16.00*
Price before profit	39.17
Desired profit	4.80 ($6 x .80*)
Desired selling price	$43.97

* Calculated as follows: With a machine output of 1.25 units per hour, .80 of a machine hour is needed to produce 1 unit; the required contribution per-machine-hour is $20; therefore, $20 x .80 = $16.

If Mr. Gail is to get a 10 percent return on his investments before taxes, the selling price must be $43.97

But suppose competitive factors mean that Mr. Gail cannot sell product C at $43.97. In such a case, he might:

Not make product C if he can use the machine time to manufacture another product which will give his company its profit of 10 percent - provided, of course, that he has orders for the second product.

Reduce the selling price, if refusing orders for product C means that the machines will be idle. Any price greater than $39.17 will generate some profit which is better than no profit.

But suppose that $39.17 is also too high. Should Mr. Gail turn down all orders for product C at less than $39.17? Not necessarily. If he has no orders to run on the machines, he should accept orders for product C at less than $39.17 because $16 of that price area contributes to manufacturing and non-manufacturing overhead. He has to pay these costs even when the machines are idle.

Keep in mind that the direct costing method of setting a price gives you flexibility. For example, Mr. Gail has to get $43.97 for product C in order to make his desired profit. But his price for that product can range from $23.17 to $43.97 (or higher, depending on market conditions.)

Any price above $39.17 brings in some contribution toward profit. Mr. Gail can break even at 39.17. Any price between $39.17 and $23.17 brings in some contribution toward his overhead. And in a pinch, he can sell as low as $23.17 and recover his direct cost - material and direct labor.

However, Mr. Gail must use this flexibility with care. It takes only a few transactions at $23.17 (recovering only direct costs) to keep him from maximizing profits over a 12-month period.

6. How to Find New Customers

This guide discusses new customer acquisition. Finding New customers and more sales are essential for profit and growth. The business owner-manager should have a specific program for regularly developing new accounts. This Guide presents a systematic approach to finding, getting, and keeping customers whose sales volume produces profit for you.

Developing New Customer Service

The problem of finding new customers is a common one. A frequent lament of sales managers is "we just don't have enough new accounts to provide the volume we need." In most companies a five percent improvement in sales volume will have a most favorable profit effect. It will equal or exceed, for example, a comparable percentage improvement in costs of material and services, productivity, inventory management or control of receivables.

How to acquire the accounts to provide such added volume becomes a matter of prime importance to survival and growth. In a great many businesses, small and large, the matter of new customer acquisition is approached in a haphazard, intermittent, unplanned and uncoordinated way. The results are understandably often less than satisfying, more expensive than expected, and generally inadequate from the standpoint of contribution of profit.

Useful insight into the problem of getting new customers can be obtained by considering the sales department as a purchasing function, spending company resources by investing in customers and sales volume. The controls, systems, thought, and effort devoted to finding the right source of materials, providing for the most effective delivery performance at a favorable price, is a continuing and evident management concern relative to its purchasing activities. Disciplines are established and controls are in place to measure supplier and purchasing effectiveness. Alternate bids are secured and potential suppliers critically tested for quality and service. Capital expenditures are closely evaluated. Yet the problem of investing to get a new customer, one who is expected to deliver profitable sales over an extended period of time, is often reduced to a simple charge to the sales department of "more new customers!"

In most cases the investment in customer acquisition is heavy, scattered, unmeasured, and unplanned. The moneys spent in this type of effort consist of advertising dollars, sales salaries and expenses, phones, samples, administrative time, and often expensive engineering costs.

The alternative to the shotgun approach to new customer or account development is usually less expensive and substantially more productive. It involves some straightforward initial analysis and planning inexpensive enough for the smallest business. It may likewise involve a change in attitude and emphasis that says that the business of investing in a customer ought to be a selective, investigative, consistent, and planned process, worthy of the closest attention of the managing sales executive. Finding and developing a worthwhile customer is a different objective from simply "more sales" or "more accounts."

The procedure involves ten steps, formalized to the degree necessary for the needs of the enterprise. These are:

1. Specify

2. Quantify

3. Identify

4. Qualify

5. Convince

6. Service

7. Collect

8. Measure

9. Expand

10. Repeat

The first seven are initially critical. A substantial account that does not pay is no "customer."

Specify - Getting New Customers

The first step is to decide what kind of new customer is needed. This involves a brief customer "specification." No one just buys steel or a machine tool or a truck. The kind of steel, its characteristics, its yield are matters of instant concern. Are we trying to buy a simple drill press or a numerically controlled multiple spindle processing unit? Does the truck have to carry one ton or ten tons, and what is to be hauled? Good analysis of the strengths or deficiencies of your present customer accounts can help in preparing your customer specification.

The New Customer Specification Might Read:

Must be within 100 miles. Must be potentially capable of repeat purchases of product "x" totaling $50,000 per year. Must appreciate value of service as opposed to being strictly a price buyer. May be an intermittent process operation where downtime is a critical concern. Frequent changeovers. Quality conscious buyer. Pays promptly on terms. Probably in the Standard Industrial Classification (SIC) or , (describe)

May currently be using product supplied by National or Atlas. Size indicator: at least 100 employees, reasonable in-house maintenance program, evidence of sales growth. Objective: profit contribution rate of 30 percent.

Or the Specification Might Be Simply:

Companies in the meat processing industry, in Michigan, Ohio, Indiana, Kentucky, Pennsylvania (beef, lamb, pork, fowl) engaged in slaughter and/or portion pack, handling over 100 head/day equivalent;

Or:

Independent distributors of products associated with the material handling industry in major trading centers in the southeastern region, having a sales force of no less than five, and carrying recognized domestic truck brands calling on local industry, particularly food processors. Must have repair facilities.

Quantify

How many this quarter or this year? "To provide the type of business required, two new accounts with volume potential of $50,000 each are needed in each of the remaining quarters of the year, plus five new smaller customers in each quarter with a potential of $25,000 to $30,000 annually." Or, "Need an average of three new small machine accounts each territory, each quarter, with potential of supply sales of $2,500 each per year following installation."

Comment: The new account is admittedly a necessary consideration for growth. Some businesses, however, becomes so concerned with the new account syndrome that they overlook the very real, often untapped, potential of existing accounts. By proper attention to maintenance selling, accounts on the books can be upgraded, expanded to new applications, and in effect become new for all practical purposes. The maintenance aspect of selling is often minimized because the battle has been won - the customer is on the books. Neglect gives your competitors the opportunity to develop a new account by taking away one of your customers. In most cases, developing an existing account is much less costly than acquiring a new customer.

Identify

Having specified and quantified the type and number of new customers wanted, the next step is to identify and rough screen the most likely candidates in the most direct and least expensive way.

A few days devoted to secondary research can prove rewarding. The precise method depends on the scope of the project, the number of required new accounts and the geographic area involved.

For the smaller local business, the telephone directory is an obvious, available, and well organized reference for new accounts. In fact, a study of the directories for several cities provides a fast, comprehensive, and specific source of information for the significant trading centers in a region.

Such listings display products and services offered for sale, the nature of the services offered (like wholesaling, retailing, or manufacturing), the specific location, phone, and zip code reference. If the listings are regarded as definitive of what is sold, they likewise are definitive, with a little deduction, of what such firms buy for resale or as original equipment manufacturers, or for use in their businesses. For example:

Acme Rat Exterminating Products; Rentals, Service, Parts - Rat Poison, Roach Spray, Ant Bait, Bird Repellent, Rat Guards, Animal Traps, Chimney Screens, Sprayers (all types), Electric Fly and Mosquito Killers, etc., including map, address, phone, and brands handled.

Under "Mailing Lists" the yellow pages also give substantial listings of sources who provide listings of various types, often very specific as to
Standard Industrial Classification (SIC) number, address, and names of relevant contacts. Purchase of one or more lists across the developed specification provides a fast way to be selective.

All things considered, like today's average cost of $100-$300 for an in-person industrial sales call, the time and money devoted to even modest preplanning data research is well spent.

Lists that can be bought generally key on SIC numbers that, depending on the number of classification digits, give names, size indicators, etc.

Other useful and readily available secondary sources of names are directories of associations, clubs, laboratories, manufacturer, Chamber of Commerce releases, mail order catalogs, and the like. The limit is only imposed by the extent of creative imagination of the researcher. The various desks in the federal and state offices and the public and university libraries are extremely helpful. Often license, permit, and registration data are available and useful.

Basic usage information to identify industries using forgings (by SIC number) was developed from a government report, "Census of Manufacturers." The scope of companies in those SIC groups was obtained for a specific geographic area from "County Business Patterns." A specific mailing list was then obtained from a directory publisher for specific SIC groups in those area. A rough screening of the list eliminated obvious unlikely prospects (Qualify). Two hundred phone calls were made to the remainder, asking the specific question, "How much do you buy of this type of forging?" Eighty-seven users were identified, large users were coded, and a program of selective selling on twenty-two accounts (some unsuspected users) was undertaken.

Qualify

One of the better sources of new customers among existing users of a product or service is your direct or indirect competitor.

Examination of the sales literature, catalogs, and trade releases of a competitor often reveals a pattern of distribution, a listing of good reference accounts, and often the details of best applications. Review of competitive advertising likewise points up many useful areas of concentration, selling methods, and coverage of what competitors regards to be their major markets.

Placing yourself in the role of a buyer of your own product or service is useful in identifying a competitor's influence points, likely user references, other applications that might not have occurred to you. Your own representatives can be helpful. In other words, shop around for your own product and see who else touches and end users in the distribution process. Each is a potential source of useful information. A frank discussion with some of your good customers will produce names of their competitors who might become your customers as well. Even on a limited local basis such efforts are most rewarding.

Your purchasing agent can be a most useful source of qualifying information because the agent talks to sales-reps who talk to your competitors. In the field of selling, detailed attention to your competitors' activities can be as equally rewarding as attention to your own customers from the standpoint of identifying new customer opportunities, advantages, deficiencies, and needs. The cost is reasonable - an open eye or ear.

When the list is reasonable - identified, broadly qualified and manageable the personal contact or specific qualification phase begins. This takes time, but the effort will be spent on a modest group of targets that have been screened against your broad specification, qualified roughly at minimum cost and have a high probability of productivity.

Good mailing lists tied to selected group targets can help identify new accounts. By a proper offering (i.e., to conduct a free survey, to provide a sample, to solve a specific problem, to offer a study result, to provide a modest prize for best new application, etc.,) a user response can be obtained. From these responses you can qualify the potential of prospective new accounts.

Learning more about your end users can also uncover buyer habits and identifying characteristics indicative of a larger group. For instance, return warranty or registration cards could give you this information from comments or answers to a few basic questions about the product by users. This information can be matched to a larger group, expanding your viewpoint.

Look also for customers among users of alternative products or services to yours. For example, users of plastics are currently converting to die casting for various reasons. Gray iron castings can often be converted to stamped parts or forgings. Automobile buyers are acquiring motor bikes and supermarket shoppers are buying less at the store and eating out more at fast food restaurants. Such habits may bring back some lost customers or make you vulnerable to pressures from the indirect competition.

Convincing a potential user to try your product or service is the next step after you have found and qualified your prospects. This step is the pay off for all your efforts and investment to attract qualified customers. Convincing the potential user to try your product or service is often similar to qualifying customers according to your specifications.

You search in a specific market area for customers that are stable companies with solid needs for your products or services. They will do repeat business and pay their bills. And you are able to come to terms and do business with them.

Keeping customers involves giving service, getting paid, measuring account profitability, expanding customer buying, and then repeating all the steps to get and to keep good customer accounts.

Remember, treat old customers the way you service new ones and you may not need so many new ones.

The Profit Evaluation

How did you do against the measure you set for yourself? Is the trend better? Are your new customers delivering the quality of volume that you want? Tracking your progress is very important. Let's say you were shooting for no increase in fixed costs and $70,000 more profit contribution on the bottom line from new accounts.

There is more to getting new customers than just chasing the volume they produce. Obviously the quality of the volume is more important. Measure your required standard, not just for the amount, but for the profit yield of the volume and the trend for the future.

The new customer development method proposed here emphasized the who, what, why, when and where of volume rather than merely the how much. This takes thoughtful planning, detailed research and screening and some expense but you do get profitable results.

7. How to Increase Your Productivity

The aim of this productivity management guide is to provide small business owners and managers with an overview of how company productivity can be improved. It covers what productivity is, how it is measured, and what a company can do to increase it.

Why should productivity management growth be a national concern? It is because, if too low, the Nation can neither improve its standard of living at home nor compete successfully abroad. Productivity growth affects wage negotiations, inflation rates, business decisions, exchange rates, a host of other economic, political and social conditions, and, therefore, every small business owner and manager.

The factors affecting both National and individual firm productivity are many and diverse. Nationally, changes in employment, hours worked, the educational, age and sex composition of the work force, levels of capital investment and savings, government regulations, capacity utilization, inflation, among others, all can affect, favorably or unfavorably, productivity rates.

There are many productivity factors the firm can manage. How well does the firm utilize new knowledge; is it working at an economy-of-scale level; are the employees highly motivated and loyal or is there labor unrest and high worker turnover; is the resource (human and capital) allocation maximizing established goals; and finally, what is the overall quality of the company's management? And, if management sees productivity as a problem, is there a commitment to establish a company-wide Productivity Improvement Program?

Establishing A Productivity Improvement Program

Recent studies indicate that the quality of management is the key to increasing business productivity. It is up to the managers to identify productivity problems and develop an appropriate program to solve these problems. In the past several years, many of the Nation's most successful, larger corporations have started Productivity improvement Programs (PIP). With profits slipping, their managements realized that improving productivity was the key to improving income; that only through an efficient and effective utilization of resources could they remain competitive and profitable.

The following Productivity Improvement Program outlines the key elements of programs successfully used by many companies including such giants as Honeywell, Westinghouse, GM and Ford.

Key elements of a Productivity Improvement Program (PIP):

1. Obtain Upper Management Support. Without top management support, experience shows a PIP likely will fail. The Chief Executive Officer should issue a clear, comprehensive policy statement. The statement should be communicated to everyone in the company. Top management also must be willing to allocate adequate resources to permit success.

2. Create New Organizational Components. A Steering Committee to oversee the PIP and Productivity Managers to implement it are essential. The Committee should be staffed by top departmental executives with the responsibilities of goal setting, guidance, advice, and general control. The Productivity Managers are responsible for the day-to-day activities of measurement and analysis. The responsibilities of all organizational components must be clear and well established.

3. Plan Systematically. Success doesn't just happen. Goals and objectives should be set, problems targeted and rank ordered, reporting and monitoring requirements developed, and feedback channels established.

4. Open Communications. Increasing productivity means changing the way things are done. Desired changes must be communicated. Communication should flow up and down the business organization. Through publications, meetings, and films, employees must be told what is going on and how they will benefit.

5. Involve Employees. This is a very broad element encompassing the quality of work life, worker motivation, training, worker attitudes, job enrichment, quality circles, incentive systems and much more. Studies show a characteristic of successful, growing businesses is that they develop a "corporate culture" where employees strongly identify with and are an important part of company life. This sense of belonging is not easy to engender. Through basic fairness, employee involvement, and equitable incentives, the corporate culture and productivity both can grow.

6. Measure and Analyze. This is the technical key to success for a PIP. Productivity must be defined, formulas and worksheets developed, sources of data identified, benchmark studies performed, and personnel assigned. Measuring productivity can be a highly complex task. The goal, however, is to keep it as simple as possible without distorting and depreciating the data. Measurement is so critical to success, a more detailed analysis is helpful.

Measuring Productivity

In an informal sense, productivity is getting more bang for the buck or doing the right things right. But these definitions do not help much when actual measurement is required. For that, a more mathematical approach is needed.

Productivity is a ratio, a comparison of what is produced and what is used to produce it. It compares outputs with inputs, that is, it divides outputs by inputs. Output is a physical entity - a car, a light-bulb, a typed page, or a processed pay voucher. For measurement, an output must be countable over time, a direct result of identifiable activities, and homogeneous (don't mix apples and oranges). Inputs can be classified into four types: labor, materials, capital and energy.

Each input can be used as the basis of a partial measure of productivity, depending upon circumstances. Labor productivity, for example, is measured by dividing output by hours worked, number of employees, or labor cost. Capital productivity is arrived at by dividing output by money invested or machine hours used. Materials productivity is output divided by units of materials used, units of scrap, or money spent. And energy productivity is output divided by units of energy consumed (like BTU's), or money spent.

Labor productivity (output = hours worked) is used by the government as the measure of the Nation's productivity. Many large, diversified companies, however, now use all four inputs to determine what is called Total Factor Productivity. In a purely office environment, since labor is the key input, some organizations use what is called the Administrative Productivity Index (API). It divides work output such as typing, loans serviced, clients interviewed or invoices processed by total hours worked to produce the administrative output. So the API essentially is a labor productivity measure.

Outputs and inputs can be measured in physical units or values or both. For example, an input unit for labor is hours and for value is dollars. A unit of output is the physical count of something and its value is its base selling price. If value (the dollar) is used as the basis of measurement, inflation must be accounted for to maintain a true value over time in constant dollars. Thus, all input and output values usually are tied to the Producer Price Index of each input and output (this compensates for the impact of inflation) to maintain valid input-output and value relationships in constant dollars over time. In other words, if revenues from product A increased 20% over last year, but its price increased by 8% to account for inflation, the real increase in dollar output was 12%. Yearly comparisons must be done using constant dollars. If the company mixes dollars and units, it still must deflate the dollars to maintain a valid relationship between physical quantities and value.

Another complicating aspect of measuring productivity is that not all inputs are equal and not all outputs are the same. Some production processes are more labor intensive than others; some use a variety of different labor skill (value) levels. Output products also change in quality and composition over time. So the process of weighing inputs and outputs to account for their relative values must be done before a truly accurate productivity measure is possible.

The point to remember is, whether employing a partial or total productivity measurement, whether for service or industrial application, or whether the business is large or small, all inputs and outputs must reflect constant values and true mixtures. To do this, all factors must be deflated and weighed.

One final technical consideration, productivity measurements should be indexed to facilitate comparison. Index each input and output measure to a base year and assign each measure the number 100. This makes it easier to calculate percentage changes over time.

Measuring productivity is time consuming and demanding: inputs and outputs must be defined, appropriate formulas developed, worksheets for keeping count printed, data collected, and calculations made. But the result will be more than just some numbers. Productivity measurement will provide a tool to assess the efficiency and effectiveness of the company, to forecast investment requirements, and to estimate the impact of cost increases or technological advances. The results do justify the effort required.

Industry Examples

So much for theory and mechanics. In practice, how have various businesses and industries actually gone about improving productivity? In the banking industry, for example, there has been revolution in productivity in the past decade. Through the use of computers, magnetic ink character recognition equipment, and mechanizing various repetitive operations, there has been a 50 percent reduction in labor requirements for check handling between.

Studies on the cosmetics industry show that through improved technology and by utilizing larger plants, it maintained a solid 4% annual manufacturing productivity increase. Economies-of-scale seem to have been the key factor here since plants with 500 or more employees were 37% more productive than the smaller ones. Studies on administrative productivity programs indicate that improved productivity comes from standardizing administrative procedures, streamlining operations, and increasing computer applications. These examples illustrate the importance to productivity of both advanced technology and proper management.

Different businesses use different measures of productivity. Airlines traditionally have used passengers boarded per employee and revenue ton-miles per employee as partial productivity measures. The Bell System has developed a sophisticated productivity program and integrated it into its overall budgeting and planning activities. The Bell program is worth a closer look.

Bell uses two Partial Productivity measures-volume of business per employee and number of phones served per employee. Both measure labor productivity. Bell also uses three Total Factor Productivity (TFP) measures to determine overall corporate performance.

One TFP measure emphasizes total output, the others gross and net value added.

Bell's TFP inputs are capital, labor, and materials. All are reported in current dollars, deflated, weighed, averaged, and indexed to arrive at a single Total Input Index. Because of the great variety of Bell products and services, output is measured in current revenues, not physical units. Again, the revenue dollars are deflated. All categories of revenues are then summed to arrive at a total dollar output figure. That total is indexed to arrive at a single Total Output Index. Finally, the output index number is divided by the input index number and the resulting figure is the Total Factor Productivity Index for the company. The percentage change over time in the TFP Index is Bell's key measure of the entire company's productivity.

Bell uses this TFP model to track productivity trends, to compare them with industry norms, and to plan long term. They also combine productivity with traditional financial analysis to determine the impact on net income of productivity growth, price change, and many other variables.

A wide-range of businesses, from small to the Bell System, have implemented successful productivity programs. Their experiences have shown that effective programs are thoroughly planned, technically correct, and fully communicated.

8. Lease Versus Buy Equipment Decision

Lease or buy equipment? this is the question. Small businesses have difficulty raising capital - that's no secret. This difficulty (among other reasons) has caused many to look at leasing equipment as an alternative financing arrangement for acquiring the use of assets. All types of equipment leasing-from motor vehicles to computers, from manufacturing machinery to office furniture-have become more and more attractive.

This lease vs buy analysis guide describes various aspects of the lease/buy decision. It lists advantages and disadvantages of leasing and provides a format for comparing costs of the options.

What Is a Lease?

Lease vs buy equipment - A lease is a long term agreement to rent equipment, land, buildings, or any other asset. In return for most-but not all-of the benefits of ownership, the user (lessee) makes periodic payments to the owner of the asset (lessor). The lease payment covers the original cost of the equipment or other asset and provides the lessor a profit.

Types of Leases

There are three major kinds of leases: the financial lease, the operating lease, and the sale and leaseback.

Financial leases are most common by far. A financial lease is usually written for a term not to exceed the economic life of the equipment. You will find that a financial lease usually provides that:

Periodic payments be made,

Ownership of the equipment reverts to the lessor at the end of the lease term,

The lease is non-cancellable and the lessee has a legal obligation to continue payments to the end of the term, and

The lessee agrees to maintain the equipment.

The operating lease, or "maintenance lease," can usually be canceled under conditions spelled out in the lease agreement. Maintenance of the asset is usually the responsibility of the owner (lessor). Computer equipment is often leased under this kind of lease.

The sale and leaseback is similar to the financial lease. The owner of an asset sells it to another party and simultaneously leases it back to use it for a specified term. This arrangement lets you free the money tied up in an asset for use elsewhere. You'll find that buildings are often leased this way.

You may also hear leases described as net leases or Cross leases. Under a net lease the lessee is responsible for expenses such as those for maintenance, taxes, and insurance. The lessor pays these expenses under a gross lease. Financial leases are usually net leases.

Finally, you might run across the term full payout lease. Under a full payout lease the lessor recovers the original cost of the asset during the term of the lease.

Kinds of Lessors

As the use of leasing has increased as a method for businesses to acquire the use of equipment and other assets, the number of companies in the leasing business has increased dramatically.

Commercial banks, insurance companies, and finance companies do most of the leasing. Many of these organizations have formed subsidiaries primarily concerned with equipment leasing. These subsidiaries are usually capable of making lease arrangements for almost anything.

In addition to financial organizations, there are companies which specialize in leasing. Some are engaged in general leasing, dealing with just about any kind of equipment. Others specialize in particular equipment, such as trucks or computers, for example.

Equipment manufacturers are also occasionally in the leasing business. Of course, they usually lease only the equipment they manufacture.

Advantages of Leasing Equipment

The obvious advantage to leasing is acquiring the use of an asset without making a large initial cash outlay. Compared to a loan arrangement to purchase the same equipment, a lease usually

requires no down payment, while a loan often requires 25 percent down;

Requires no restriction on a company's financial operations, while loans often do;

Spreads payments over a longer period (which means they'll be lower) than loans permit; and

Provides protections against the risk of equipment obsolescence, since the lessee can get rid of the equipment at the end of the lease.

There may also tax benefits in leasing. Lease payments are deductible as operating expenses if the arrangement is a true lease. Ownership, however, usually has greater tax advantages through depreciation. Naturally, you need to have enough income and resulting tax liability to take advantage of those two benefits.

Leasing has the further advantage that the leasing firm has acquired considerable knowledge about the kinds of equipment it leases. Thus, it can provide expert technical advice based on experience with the leased equipment.

Finally, there is one further advantage of leasing that you probably hope won't ever be of use to you. In the event of bankruptcy, claims of the lessor to the assets of a firm are more restricted than those of general creditors.

Disadvantages of Leasing

In the first place, leasing usually costs more because you lose certain tax advantages that go with ownership of an asset. Leasing may not, however, cost more if you couldn't take advantage of those benefits because you don't have enough tax liability for them to come into play.

Obviously, you also lose the economic value of the asset at the end of the lease term, since you don't own the asset. Lessees have been known to grossly underestimate the salvage value of an asset. If they had known this value from the outset, they might have decided to buy instead of lease.

Further, you must never forget that a lease is a long-term legal obligation. Usually you can't cancel a lease agreement. So, it you were to end an operation that used leased equipment, you might find you'd still have to pay as much as if you had used the equipment for the full term of the lease.

Accounting Treatment of Leases

Historically, financial leases were "off the balance sheet" financing. That is, lease obligations often were not recorded directly on the balance sheet, but listed in footnotes, instead. Not explicitly accounting for leases frequently resulted in a failure to state operational assets and liabilities fairly.

The Financial Accounting Standards Board (FASB), the rule-making body of the accounting profession, required that capital leases be recorded on the balance sheet as both an asset and a liability. This was in recognition of the long-term nature of a lease obligation.

Cost Analysis of Lease v. Loan/Purchase

You can analyze the costs of the lease versus purchase problem through discounted cash flow analysis. This analysis compares the cost of each alternative by considering: the timing of the payments, tax benefits, the interest rate on a loan, the lease rate, and other financial arrangements.

To make the analysis you must first make certain assumptions about the economic life of the equipment, salvage value, and depreciation.

A straight cash purchase using a firm's existing funds will almost always be more expensive than the lease or loan/buy options because of the loss of use of the funds. Besides, most small firms don't have the large amounts of cash needed for major capital asset acquisitions in the first place.

To evaluate a lease you must first find the net cash outlay (not cash flow) in each year of the lease term. You find these amounts by subtracting the tax savings from the lease payment. This calculation gives you the net cash outlay for each year of the leases.

Each year's net cash outlay must next be discounted to take into account the time value of money. This discounting gives you the present value of each of the amounts.

The present value of an amount of money is the sum you would have to invest today at a stated rate of interest to have that amount of money at a specified future date. Say someone offered to give you $100 five years from now. How much could you take today and be as well off?

Common sense tells you you could take less than $100, because you'd have the use of the money for the five year period. Naturally, how much less you could take depends on the interest rate you thought you could get if you invested the lesser amount. For example, to have $100 five years from now at six percent compounded annually, you'd have to invest $74.70 today. At 10 percent, you could take $62.10 now and have the $100 at the end of five years.

Fortunately there are tables which provide the discount factors for present value calculations. There are also relatively inexpensive special purpose pocket calculators programmed to make these calculations.

Why bother with making these present value calculation? Well, you've got to make them to compare the actual cash flows over the time periods. You simply can't realistically compare methods of financing without taking into account the time value of money. It may seem confusing and complex at first, but if you work through an example, you'll begin to see that the technique isn't difficult-just sophisticated.

Evaluation of the borrow/buy option is a little more complicated because of the tax benefits that go with ownership, loan interest deductions, and depreciation.

As noted earlier, the salvage value is one of the advantages of ownership. It must be considered in making the comparison. Naturally, it s possible that salvage costs for real asset could be very high or be next to nothing. Salvage value assumptions need to be made carefully.

Thus, while this sort of analysis is useful, you can't make a lease/buy decision solely on cost analysis figures. The advantages and disadvantages discussed earlier, while tough to qualify, may outweigh differences in cost-especially if costs are reasonably close.

Look Before You Lease

A lease agreement is a legal document. It carries a long term obligation. You must be thoroughly informed of just what you're committing yourself to. Find out the lessor's financial condition and reputation. Be reasonably sure that the lease arrangements are the best you can get, that the equipment is what you need, and that the term is what you want. Remember, once the agreement is struck, it's just about impossible to change it.

The lease document will spell out the precise provisions of the agreement. Agreements may differ, but the major items will include:

The specific nature of the financing agreement,

Payment amount,

Term of agreement,

Disposition of the asset at the end of the term,

Schedule of the value of the equipment for insurance and settlement purposes in case of damage or destruction,

Who is responsible for maintenance and taxes,

Renewal options,

Cancellation penalties, and

Special provisions.

9. How to Fix Production Mistakes

This guide is intended for small manufacturers and deals with the essential issues and steps that should be considered by a manufacturer when a production mistake has been found. A production error is analyzed in check-list form to establish its extent and its effect on the product and the production line and the steps needed for corrective action that integrates the "fix" into the existing production systems and schedules.

What Will You Do?

What would you do if several or several hundred production units manufactured in your plant were found to incorporate a defective or improperly installed component? Assume the logical complication that the defective units had been distributed to numerous work stations along the production line to be fitted into higher assemblies. Add to this the grim fact that defective end items had been shipped from your plant and were now in the transportation pipeline, at your dealers, and in the hands of consumers.

Production mistakes are not unique. To the contrary, they are chronic. They cost industry hundreds of millions of dollars each year, and they waste resources that are becoming increasingly scarce. When you, the manufacturer make a production mistake, we all lose. The ultimate frustration occurs when managers and their people are not sure what needs to be done to correct the problem. When the corrective action process is unorganized or in disarray, the drain on resources is enormous and unpredictable. The ultimate cost of the fix soars.

Production mistakes are a challenge to a good manager's sense of order. Correction is vital to the survival of the company. Actions need to be taken and controlled to reestablish quality production.

The following questions are far from all inclusive. Each product and plant has its own characteristics, and fixing a production mistake would, of necessity, need to be tailored to both. However, the questions and the outline of a corrective action plan should stimulate your thinking and help you to organize your people and resources should you be confronted with a production mistake.

Analysis

1. Do you know the exact physical nature of the mistake?

Did a part break?

Was a circuit incomplete?

Was an incorrect material used?

Do you know what happened?

2. Have you examined physical evidence of the

mistake?

Will a personal examination of the mistake by you help you to understand the problem better?

3. Do you know where in the plant the mistake actually occurred?

Have you pinpointed and brought to the attention of management the specific work unit and work station where the error was first noticed?

Did you track back along the production line to the work station and worker where the mistake was being made?

Did you track the mistake forward along the production system to ascertain the extent to which the fault was included in higher assemblies and end items?

4. Did you stop the work step that was creating the mistake?

5. Did you identify the people, skills, materials, tools and equipment, data or work practices that caused the mistake?

Do you know which were directly responsible?

Do you know which were indirect contributors?

Do you know how they became part of the approved production process?

6. Must you correct the mistake on finished items or

on items on which rework would be economically or technologically unprofitable or impractical? In answering this question, have you considered:

Safe use of the final product by the ultimate consumer?

Established quality standards?

The effect on service life?

Maintainability of the part during normal operations?

The effect on the cost of operating the end item?

Other significant characteristics included in the specifications?

7. If the error will not cause significant deviations from drawings or specifications, should you review the situation with the ordering agencies or companies before taking any further action on those items that now incorporate the defect?

8. Should you impose a work stoppage?

Do you know what the effects of a work stoppage will be on:

Your production line?

Your contractual commitments?

Do you have alternate workloads that can be readily injected into the gaps until a corrective action decision for the mistake can be implemented?

9. Have parts, assemblies or end items, incorporating the error, been shipped from your plant? If they have:

Have you estimated the effects of the mistake on the market place?

Have you estimated the effects of a decision to recall the defective items from your customers, dealers or consumers?

Are trucks or freight cars now being loaded by your shipping department with items that contain the production error?

Should the shipments be off-loaded?

Have you issued instructions to cover the situation?

Have you confirmed that your instructions were complied with?

Do you know the effect of the stop shipment order on the customers scheduled to receive the items?

Do they have sufficient stocks on hand that do not contain the mistake to tide them over the rework period?

Can you identify all shipments of the items that have the production error, by customers' identity, shipping order number, item serial numbers, method/date/time of shipment, and any other means of identification that will assist your customers to locate the faulty items and segregate them from usable stocks in their warehouses, dealers shelves or in actual use?

10. Based on your analysis to this point, should the recipients of items containing the production error be notified?

If notification is to be made, have you issued the required instructions, including the recording of the means of notification, date/time/method, and the names of the persons initiating the contract and receiving the message.

Are you certain the message was received by the customer and understood?

If you have imposed a work stoppage on the production line, and stopped further shipments of the items, do you know your shipping commitments for the next 24 hours, 48 hours, 72 hours?

Should the recipients of the shipping commitments in (the preceding question) be notified of the delay in shipping and given a new shipping date?

11. If the faulty items are to be recalled to the plant, can shipments in the pipeline be diverted back?

If they can be, have you arranged for temporary storage space?

As an alternative to recalling the items back to the plant, can the shipments be completed and arrangements made with your customers for the rework, either by doing it themselves or by contracting out?

As another alternative, can you send technicians from your plant to your customers facility to fix the error?

Have you examined the alternatives to correct defective items that were shipped and arrived at the most logical and practicable course of action considering your customer's needs, the time factors involved, the economics of the situation, and your reputation?

Do you know what the effects will be of your decision to fix or not to fix?

Taking Action

1. If the mistake is to be fixed, do you know what needs to be done to develop the corrective action and put it into effect?

2. Have you considered the demands that will be made on and the availability of:

Plant facilities (structural and environmental) Finances?

Energy sources?

Communications systems?

Transportation?

Public relations and Marketing?

Shop equipment?

Materials?

Supplies?

Tools?

Data?

People (skills, training, safety, work-hours, etc.)?

Other services?

3. Can the faulty items be processed economically for tear down to get at the error and then re-injected into your routine production system without disrupting the production flow?

If not, do you need a special, one-time production group to do the tear down, repair and reassembly job?

If, after tear down, the parts can be re-injected into routine production, have you identified the points along the production system where each identifiable part or partial assembly can be inserted?

4. Have you identified all the work units and work stations that will be directly affected by the rework of the faulty items and the corrective action in general?

Do you know how they will be affected?

Do the supervisors and direct workers of those work units and at those work stations understand the problem and what is expected of them?

Have you ascertained which work units or work stations

can be by-passed during the fix to minimize disruption to normal production and reduce the ultimate cost impact?

5. Will the fix make it necessary to:

Realign work space?

Move shop equipment?

Modify tools and equipment

Fabricate jigs and special holding devices?

Redesign parts?

Revise procedures?

Change standards?

Retrain people?

Reschedule and Reprogram?

Modify contracts with customers?

6. Can the corrective action taken as a result of finding this error be applied to future designs, management practices and production system improvements anywhere else in the plant?

Has this experience given you ideas to improve your operations?

General Characteristics of a Corrective Action Plan

A corrective action should be planned out and integrated

into your production control system, which could be Gantt Charting (a bar chart) or the Critical Path Method (a graphic model). Both systems aid production planning and scheduling by setting up time schedules for starting and finishing various tasks on one or many items. Your corrective action plan form requires careful completion according to the following nine steps:

1) Problem: A concise statement of the problem. References can be included to identify other documents giving more detailed information.

2) Work Unit (Prime): The title or other identifying symbol of the shop, unit or group where the cause of the problem exists and where the action will be taken. A mistake may be quite extensive and the effects fragmented and widespread. Actions may be needed by several work units. A sub-plan may be appropriate for the different work units, functions or locations.

3) Work Unit (Associated): The prime work unit usually needs help from other units. It may be useful to identify these supporting units, their supervisors and telephone numbers. It can save time for those directly involved in the action.

4) Date: The date the plan was approved can provide a valuable control device. The plan may need to be revised to include additional steps, delete certain actions, or change procedures even as the action proceeds. The DATE plus a note that the sheet supersedes one of a prior DATE is the control.

The next three Blocks represent the Task Breakdown. It may be more logical to break the actions down by work station; worker in some situations; in other cases the "Start/Completion Date" may be the most important factor in sequencing the steps. Circumstances may dictate that accessibility to certain parts on the assembly compels the sequence. Each situation and set of circumstances would need to be analyzed in detail to arrange the best sequence.

5) Work Station/Responsible Worker: Who does what, and in what sequence? The station and worker should he in the WORK UNIT identified at the top of the page.

6) Operations: To the most practicable extent this space should state the specific actions that needed to be taken-sequentially if possible. Generalizations should he avoided as they might be subjected to varying interpretations and lead to confusion. This should not be the place to say why the mistake happened or otherwise analyze the problem. This space should confine itself to do-this type instructions. It should be of DIRECT use to the worker doing the job.

7) Starting /Completion Dates: The dates should be realistic, otherwise, a work stoppage could occur. The dates should consider such diverse factors as the availability of tools and equipment, test sets, raw materials, energy, skills, work-hours and work shifts. It could consider whether or not the dates would be compatible with normal production operations. If new design or fabrication techniques are to be applied, the starting dates could be affected accordingly. A START and COMPLETION date would ordinarily be required for each entry under OPERATIONS.

8) Follow-Up Date: Follow-up is an option of management to assure that the action was taken and was adequate. It could include examining the product, checking documentation or interviews with the people doing the work. It assures the manager that the job was done, and done right.

9) Confirm Permanent Correction: After the crisis has passed, management may wish to take that extra step that would prevent the mistake from recurring. What really caused the problem? What should be done about it? Is a permanent change needed in tools, equipment or materials? Should the shop layout be changed? Do workers need additional training? What about quality control and product inspection procedures? The fact that a mistake occurred in one unit could mean that it might happen in another. The mistake that was corrected could provide an opportunity for a significant technical or management improvement throughout the plant.

10. The Equipment Replacement Decision

The parts replacement decision, to replace a piece of equipment should be based on facts and figures. The judgment which the owner-manager of a small company makes should be the result of weighing the costs of keeping the old equipment against the cost of its replacement.

This parts replacement guide discusses the elements involved in making such a cost comparison. Examples are used to illustrate the gathering and use of the appropriate cost figures.

Sooner or later, you must decide whether you should keep an existing unit of equipment or replace it with a new unit. As time goes by, equipment deteriorates and becomes obsolete. Frequent breakdowns occur, defective output increases, unit labor costs rise, and production schedules cannot be met. At some point, these occurrences become serious enough to cause you to wonder whether or not you should replace the equipment.

The problem is that the new equipment costs money, and the question that comes to you is: Will the advantages of the new equipment be great enough to justify the investment it requires?

You answer this question by making a cost comparison.

To recognize the better alternative you need to know the total cost of each alternative - keeping the old equipment or buying a replacement. Once these costs are determined, you can compare them and identify the more economical equipment. The paragraphs that follow discuss the individual costs which you must consider when computing the total cost of the old and new equipment.

Depreciation

One of the costs connected with any type of equipment is depreciation. For cost comparison purposes, depreciation is simply the amount by which an asset decreases in value over some period of time. For example, if you bought a piece of equipment for $20,000 and sold it for $6,000 after seven years of service, you would say that the depreciation during the seven-year period was $20,000 minus $6,000, or $14,000. This $14,000 was one of your costs of owning the equipment for that period.

From this, it follows that when considering equipment replacement, you must calculate the future depreciation expense that you will experience with both the old and the new equipment.

Insofar as the new equipment is concerned, this calls for knowing certain things about the equipment. You need to know (1) its first cost, (2) its estimated service life, and (3) its expected salvage value. The difference between the first cost and the salvage value will represent the amount by which the equipment will depreciate during its life - that is, during the time you expect to use it.

You determine the depreciation expense for the old equipment in the same general way but for one import difference. The difference is that no expenditure is required to procure the equipment because you already own it. However, a decision to keep it does require an investment at the present time. This investment is equal to the asset's market value - that is, to the amount of money the asset would bring in if it were replaced and sold. If this amount is not equal to the equipment's book value. the depreciation expense that was shown for accounting purposes is in error because it did not reflect the actual depreciation.

So to determine the actual future depreciation expense that will be experienced with the old equipment, you must know (1) its present market value, (2) its estimated remaining service life, and (3) its expected salvage value at the end of that life. The difference between the present market value and the future salvage value represents the amount by which the equipment will depreciate during its remaining life in your business.

To sum up, you must begin your cost comparison by determining the first cost of the new equipment and estimating its service life and salvage value. Also, you must determine the market value of the old equipment and estimate its remaining service life and future salvage value.

Interest

In addition to depreciation, every piece of equipment generates an interest expense. This expense occurs because owning an asset ties up some of your capital. If you had to borrow this capital you would have to pay for the use of the money. This "out-of-pocket" cost is one of the costs of owning the equipment.

The story is the same even when you use your own money. In this case, the amount involved is no longer available for other investments which could bring you a return. This "opportunity cost" is one of the costs of owning the equipment.

To cite an example, suppose that the market value of an asset during a given year is $10,000. Suppose also that at the same time, you are getting capital at a cost of 15 percent per year. On the other hand, suppose that if you converted the asset into cash, you could invest the money and realize a rate of return of 15 percent per year. In either case, a decision to own that asset during that year would be costing you 15 percent of $10,000, or $1,500 in interest.

Thus, in any comparison of equipment alternatives, you must take the cost of money into account. So, when determining whether or not existing equipment should be replaced, you must estimate what money is costing you in terms of a percent per year.

Operating Costs

There is a third type of cost - the cost of operation - that is experienced with a piece of equipment. Typical operating cost are expenditures for labor, materials, supervision, maintenance, and power.

These cost must be considered because your choice of equipment affects them. You may find it convenient to estimate these costs on an annual basis. You can get figures for each unit of equipment by estimating its next-year operating costs as well as the annual rate at which these costs are likely to increase as wage rates rise and the equipment deteriorates.

For example, you might say that operating cost for the new equipment are likely to be $16,000 during the first year of its life. You might also estimate that after the first year, the operating costs will increase at a rate of $500 a year.

You can simplify the problem of estimating these costs by either (1) ignoring those costs that are the same for the old and the new equipment or (2) estimating only the differences between the operating costs of the two units. With this simplification, the total costs which you calculate for each type of equipment will be understated by the same amount. Therefore, the difference between these total costs will remain the same, and you will still be able to recognize the more economical alternative.

Revenues

Often, the revenues generated by the old and the new equipment will be the same. When this is true, revenues can be ignored for the same reason that you can ignore equal operating costs.

But if revenues are affected by the choice of equipment, they must be considered. For example, you might estimate that the higher quality of output from the new equipment will increase annual sales by $1,200. You can handle this difference in revenues in either of two ways.

One way is to show the $1,200 as an additional annual cost that will be experienced with the old equipment.

The other way is to treat the $1,200 as a negative annual cost and associate it with the new equipment. The total cost which you calculate will be affected by your choice of method, but the difference between these cost will remain the same.

An Annual Average Cost

In brief, you can make the necessary cost analysis on the new and old equipment only after you have the proper data for each. For the new equipment, the data include first cost, service life, salvage value, operating costs, and revenue advantage. For the old equipment, the data include market value, remaining service life, future salvage value, and operating costs. In addition, for both alternatives, the cost of money must be stated in the form of an interest rate.

By using these data, you can determine the elements of the total costs. These elements consist of depreciation expense, interest expense, operating costs, and possibly lost revenues. Now, it so happens that these costs can be expressed in a variety of ways.

However, the simplest way for cost comparison purposes is to describe these cost elements in terms of an average annual cost. Doing so permits you to calculate and compare the total average annual costs of the old and new equipment and reach a decision.

How these costs can be computed is shown in the example that follows.

The Old Equipment

Look first at some facts about an old piece of equipment. It has a market value of $7,000. If retained, its service life is expected to be four years, and its salvage value is expected to be $1,000. Next-year operating costs are estimated to be $8,000 but will probably increase at an annual rate of $200. The cost of money is 12 percent per year. With this set of figures, you can obtain the total average annual cost of the alternative of keeping this equipment.

Annual Depreciation Expense. You begin by calculating the equipment's average annual depreciation expense. You do this by determining the total depreciation and dividing that amount by the asset's four-year life. Your answer is $1,500 which you get as follows:

Annual depreciation =

$$\frac{\$7,000 - \$1,000}{4} = \$1,500$$

Annual Interest Expense. Next, you calculate the average annual interest expense. The maximum investment in the equipment is $7,000, its present market value. But as time goes by, the investment in the asset decreases because its market value decreases. The minimum investment is reached at the end of the equipment's life when it has a salvage value of $1,000. The average investment will be the average of these maximum and minimum values. You calculate it

Average investment =

$$\frac{\$7,000 + \$1,000}{2} = \$4,000$$

To determine the average annual interest expense, you multiply the average investment ($4,000, in this example) by the annual interest rate of 12 percent. Doing so yields:

Annual Interest = $4,000 x .12 = $480

Annual Operating Costs. You can determine the average annual operating costs by computing the average of the individual annual operating costs. In this example, they are estimated to be $8,000, $8,200, $8,400, and $8,600. The average for these figures is $8,300 which you obtain as follows:

Annual operating costs =

$$\frac{\$8,000 + \$8,200 + \$8,400 + \$8,600}{4} = \$8,300$$

Total Average Annual Cost. For the old equipment, the total average annual cost is simply the sum of the calculated average annual cost for: (1) depreciation, (2) interest, and (3) operating expenses. This sum is $10,280, as shown below.

Item Average annual cost

Depreciation	$1,500
Interest	480
Operating Costs	8,300
Total	$10,280

The New Equipment

Look now at the facts on a piece of new equipment which may be a replacement for the old equipment. The first cost of this new equipment is $30,000. Its life is estimated to be ten years, and it will probably have a salvage value of $6,000. Operating costs with this equipment are expected to average $5,200 a year. Furthermore, it is estimated to have an annual revenue advantage of $300 over the old equipment. The cost of money is 12 percent per year.

You use the same approach as you did for the old equipment to determine the total average annual cost of this new equipment.

Annual Depreciation Expense. You start with the average annual depreciation expense and find it to be $2,400, as follows:

Annual depreciation =

$$\frac{\$30,000 - \$6,000}{10} = \$2,400$$

Annual Interest Expense. You multiply the average investment in this asset by the interest rate to obtain the average annual interest expense. The average investment is $18,000 (one-half of the sum of the $30,000 first cost and the $6,000 salvage value). The average annual interest expense is $2,160 obtained as follows:

Annual interest = .5 ($30,000 + $6,000) x.12 = $2,160

Total Average Annual Cost. When you also take the estimated operating costs and revenue advantage into account, you find the total average annual cost to be $9,460, as shown below.

Item Average annual cost

Depreciation	$2,400
Interest	2,160
Operating Costs	5,200
	$9,760
Less: Revenue advantage	300
	$9,460

The Comparison

When you have the total average annual cost for the old and the new equipment, you are ready to compare the two. In the example, the calculated annual cost is $10,280 for the old equipment and $9,460 for the new. On the surface, the new equipment is more economical than the old. But is it?

You may argue that with the old equipment you are committing yourself for only four years, whereas with the new, your commitment is for ten years. This fact suggests a need for considering the kind of equipment that may be available for replacement purposes four years from now as compared with ten years from now.

But no one can forecast that far into the future. It is best to ignore the nature of future replacements in your computations and assume that the replacement available four years from now will have the same annual cost as the one available ten years from now.

Irreducible Factors

When your calculated annual costs show that the one unit of equipment has a decided advantage over the other, you can usually select the better alternative by comparing these calculated costs. But what do you do when the annual costs of the old and the new equipment do not differ greatly? In such a case, you should consider the fact that the estimates might contain errors and that there are things on which a dollar value cannot be placed.

So you may have to base your decision on irreducible factors - factors that cannot be reduced to dollars and cents.

A few examples will suggest the nature of such factors.

First, if total average annual costs are about the same, you will probably favor the equipment that required the smaller investment and has the shorter life. The same will hold true when you suspect that technological advances will result in more efficient equipment becoming available in the near future.

As another example, you will prefer the equipment which has greater output capacity, safety, and reliability even though the value of these is unknown.

And finally, when you suspect that interest rates and the price of new equipment will increase significantly, you will be inclined to invest in new equipment now rather than later.

11. How to Set Up a Quality Control System

This guide presents a sample quality control system closely prepared from one developed by Honeywell, Inc. It may be used as a guide in initiating your own quality assurance system, whether you sell to consumers, industrial users, or government.

Basic Quality Elements

All quality control and inspection systems have simple, basic elements in common:

Organization - setting and assigning specific authority and responsibility for each phase of the system;

Quality Planning - writing work instructions with realistic "defect prevention" rules, looking at manufacturing processes for possible quality trouble spots, setting acceptance/rejection standards, controlling accepted/rejected products, and setting up a means of using suppliers' and customers' failure information to improve product quality;

Product Specification Control - making sure everyone always has the latest technical data for properly producing, inspecting, and shipping the product;

Supplier Product Quality Control - watching purchases to make sure that the people you buy from know and observe your quality requirements as well as technical specifications;

Measurement and Test Equipment Control - setting up a system to insure that such equipment is properly and regularly calibrated to established standards;

Nonconforming Material Control - spotting defects as early in production as possible and keeping faulty items from reaching customers; and

Records and Reports - setting up a system that tracks all steps of the production, inspection, and shipping cycle to identity existing and potential problem areas.

The following sample manual incorporates these basics. It may be adapted to fit your needs. It is recommended that each section of a manual you work up be on a loose-leaf sheet for easy reference and revision. Remember, the best manual in the world won't do any good unless every employee - not just those in Quality Assurance - is convinced that producing quality products is of prime importance.

A Sample Manual

Introduction

This manual describes for our employees and customers our quality control system. The system applies both to the items we produce and to the items we buy from our suppliers.

As dictated by the complexity of product design, manufacturing techniques used, and customer requirements, more specific written procedures may be required to implement the policies set in this manual.

No changes may be made to this manual or any supplementary quality control procedures unless approved by the plant manager or an authorized representative.

Table of Contents

Description Section

Appendix A Organization Chart

Appendix B Purchase Order Form

Appendix C Inspection Data Form

(Each company should use its own forms for the Appendices).

Appendix D Identification Tags

Appendix E Travel Card

1.0 Scope

1.1 The quality control system includes: receiving, identifying, stocking and issuing parts and material; all manufacturing processes; packing, storing; and shipping.

1.2 The system is designed to ensure customer satisfaction through quality control management of supplies made and services performed here, and by our suppliers at their facilities. It is designed to spot processing problems early so we can correct them before we've produced a lot of faulty items.

1.3 Written inspection and test procedures will be prepared to supplement drawings and other specifications, as necessary.

2.0 Responsibilities

2.1 The supervisor of quality assurance reports directly to the plant manager.

2.2 The quality assurance supervisor's responsibilities include:

2.2.1 Planning how to meet customer's quality requirements

2.2.2 Reviewing customer drawings and specifications.

2.2.3 Determining inspection points.

2.2.4 Writing inspection and test instructions.

2.2.5 Establishing (and making sure employees follow) the most effective and efficient quality assurance procedures possible.

2.2.6 Keeping adequate quality assurance records.

2.2.7 Reviewing quality assurance records and overseeing follow-up for correction and prevention of defects.

2.2.8 Assuring that our suppliers' quality control and follow-up are adequate.

2.2.9 Inspecting all special and standard gages, test equipment, and tooling used to manufacture products when we acquire them and calibrating them on a regularly scheduled basis.

2.2.10 Coordinating in-plant correction of items rejected by customers, explaining to customers what action will be taken, and evaluating the actions for effectiveness.

2.2.11 Making sure inspectors make unbiased decisions to accept or reject items.

3.0 Purchase Order Control

3.1 All of our purchase orders to suppliers must be approved by the plant manager or an authorized representative.

3.2 When the purchase order is released, our buyer will send our supplier all required drawings, specifications, and other customer requirements (such as material or process certifications, physical or chemical analysis, source inspections) with the purchase order.

3.3 If there is a drawing or specification change after our order is placed with the supplier, our buyer will send the supplier a purchase order change, including our latest Engineering change and the latest drawings or other specifications.

3.4 Copies of all purchase orders will be kept on file for our customers to review.

4.0 Drawing and Specification Change Control

4.1 We manufacture to customer drawings and specifications. Sets of these are filed in job number folders in Production Control files.

4.2 Production Control is responsible for charging out and keeping track of drawings and specifications.

4.3 The Sales Department receives Engineering changes from our customers and is responsible for sending these changes to Production Control immediately.

4.4 Production Control is responsible for issuing the latest Engineering changes, drawings, and specifications of departments that need them and for voiding outdated Engineering changes, drawings, and specifications.

4.5 A standard procedure will be set up to control changes by effective date or serial/lot number.

5.0 Receiving Inspection

5.1 All parts and materials will be received and logged in by the Receiving Department.

5.2 All parts and materials will be sent to Receiving Inspection after logging in.

5.3 Receiving Inspection will assure that proper certification, physical and chemical test data, special process certifications, or source inspection certifications are with the items to be inspected.

5.4 The receiving inspector must document the complete results of all inspection and tests.

5.5 Inspection will identify accepted lots and send them to stock.

5.6 Rejected lots will be identified and set aside in Receiving Inspection until the buyer and Production Control decide on disposition.

5.7 The Receiving Department will send a copy of each rejection report to the Purchasing Department and the supplier.

5.8 The Purchasing Department has the responsibility of assuring that a pattern of continually receiving faulty items from any supplier doesn't develop and assuring supplier corrective action.

5.9 The Quality Department will follow-up to see that a supplier who has sent us items we reject has effectively corrected what it has been doing wrong.

5.10 Receiving Inspection instructions will be written with consideration given to the complexity of the parts, material received, and customer requirements. Follow customer instructions (if any) for inspection.

5.11 Sample according to customer requirements (if any).

5.12 The Quality Department will review Receiving Inspection records periodically to see if any suppliers are consistently failing to meet standards.

5.13 All inspection records will show the number inspected, the number rejected, and the name of the inspector.

5.14 Inspection records will also show the disposition of supplier-provided records and data.

6.0 Raw Material Control

6.I Raw materials, bar stock, sheet stock, and castings will be marked so they can be traced to their certification, and stored in an area apart from the normal flow of in-process material.

6.2 Copies of all certifications will be filed in the job order number folder by job order number and available for customer review.

6.3 Only raw material accepted by Receiving Inspection will be released for production.

6.4 Certified stock will be issued from its storage area only for job order requirements.

6.5 Verification of suppliers' certifications will be ordered from independent testing laboratories when deemed necessary by the Quality Department or to meet our customers' requirements.

6.6 All certifications will be traceable to purchase order, date of receipt of the material, and the inspector of the material.

In Process Inspection

7.1 The Quality Department will make first piece inspection after set up is completed and approved by Production.

7.2 No production runs will be made until first piece inspection is accepted.

7.3 After first piece inspection acceptance, in-process inspections will be made by the Quality Department at intervals adequate for early detection of processes producing material that doesn't meet standards.

7.4 The Quality Department will keep records of all first piece and in-process inspections.

7.5 The inspection records will be stored in the job number folder and will be available for customer review.

7.6 Tag or otherwise identify rejected items and move them to an area apart from the normal flow of in-process materials.

7.7 The Quality Department will follow-up to prevent recurrence of faulty material.

7.8 Inspection records will list: the number of pieces accepted, the number rejected, kind of defects and basic causes of rejection, date of inspection, and the inspector's name.

7.9 Attachment shows the locations of fabrication and inspection stations. For each station, it lists the types of items subject to inspection, the kind of inspection done, and the applicable drawings and specifications.

7.10 Special processes will require appropriate inspections and controls, including qualification and certification of personnel and equipment.

8.0 Assembly Inspection and Functional Testing

8.1 Production personnel will make assembly inspections and do functional testing, as required.

8.2 The Quality Department will check functional test under an established sampling plan.

8.3 The Quality Department will keep the inspection records.

8.4 The inspection records will be kept in the job number folder and will be available for customer review.

8.5 All faulty (discrepant) assemblies will be marked and set apart so they won't be accidentally used.

8.6 The Quality Department will initiate corrective and follow-up action to prevent recurrence of faulty material.

8.7 Inspection records will list: the number accepted, the number rejected, the date of the inspection, and the inspector's name.

9.0 Final inspection and Testing

9.1 Final inspection and tests will be performed either on 100 percent or on a sample of the items. The number of items sampled will depend on the complexity of the items and customer requirements. Inspection will follow either customer-supplied procedures when available or MIL-STD-105D.

9.2 Each end item will be inspected/tested 100 percent, unless the customer asks otherwise.

9.3 The Quality Department will keep all final inspection and test records.

9.4 Inspection and test records will be filed in the job number folder and will be available for customer review,

9.5 The Quality Department will follow-up to see that processes producing faulty materials are corrected and to prevent recurrence of faulty material from those processes.

9.6 All faulty material will be marked and set apart from the normal flow of finished material.

9.7 Faulty material will not be shipped to the customer without specific customer instructions to submit such Nonconforming material.

9.8 Rejected material which has been repaired, reworked, or sorted must be resubmitted to final inspection to make sure it meets requirements.

9.9 Inspection records will list: the number of pieces accepted, the number rejected, the date of inspection; and the inspector's name.

10.0 Faulty (Discrepant) Material Control

10.1 All faulty (Nonconforming) material, supplies, or parts will be placed in a "DO NOT USE" area. The items will be clearly marked with job number, part number, revision letter, lot size, defect, inspector's name, and any other information necessary.

10.2 The specific reason an item has been rejected will be clearly written on a rejection tag attached to each part or container.

10.3 No one may remove items from the "DO NOT USE" area until disposition is determined by a Material Review Board made up of the plant manager, and representatives of the Production and Quality Departments.

10.4 Nonconforming material will not be shipped unless the customer's buyer approves it. The shipping documents will be marked with what's wrong with the items.

10.5 The Quality Department will control all lots submitted for acceptance inspection. Each lot will be kept as a unit, apart from other lots, and out of the normal flow of material.

10.6 During the processing of material all production and inspection operations must be kept in proper order. Each step must be completed before the next step is begun.

10.7 The Quality Department will set up a system so that the stage of inspection each item is in, can easily be identified.

10.8 Unidentified material will be taken out of the normal flow of production until it is inspected to insure that it meets all specifications.

10.9 Reworked material will be segregated from other material until the Quality Department determines its status.

11.0 Tool and Gage Control

11.1 All special tools, jigs, fixtures, gages, and measuring equipment must be properly identified,

11.2 Each new or reworked tool, jig, fixture, gage, and item of measuring equipment will be inspected before issue for use.

11.3 All gages, measuring and test equipment will be calibrated to standards.

11.4 A written schedule for calibrating gages, measuring and test equipment will be set and strictly followed. Frequency of calibration will be based on type and purpose of the equipment and severity of usage.

11.5 A restricted area for storing and calibrating gages, measuring, and test equipment will be set up.

11.5.1 A strict system of issue, control, and return will be set and followed.

11.6 If the customer supplies special gages, they will be checked at the intervals the customer sets. If the customer supplies no inspection schedule, the equipment will be checked according to a schedule that takes into account type, purpose, and severity of use.

11.7 Calibration will follow the written procedures kept in the calibration area.

11.8 Obsolete or out-of service tools and gages will be tagged.

11.9 Decals or stickers will be put on tools and gages or their containers to show the last date of calibration and the due date of the next calibration.

11.10 Personal, as well as company-0wned production and inspection tools, must be properly and regularly calibrated.

12.0 Overrun Stock Control

12.1 The Quality Department will oversee overrun stock.

12.2 The Quality Department will insure that any overrun parts sent to stock are properly marked "accepted." The part number, latest drawing number and specification revision, date of inspection, job number, and quantity of parts will be shown. The Quality Department will periodically check to see that the parts are properly packed to prevent deterioration and damage.

12.3 No overrun parts will be shipped to a customer until they are reinspected and found in acceptable condition and to meet the latest drawing and specification revisions.

13.0 Packing and Shipping

13.1 No order will be shipped to a customer until all shipping papers are stamped or signed and dated by the final inspector.

13.2 No order will be shipped until all required certifications, test reports, special samples, etc., have been packed with the material in accordance with the customer's requirements and accepted by the final inspector.

13.3 All material will be packed to prevent damage deterioration, and substitution.

13.4 The customer will be identified on the packaging, parts, and as otherwise necessary to prevent lost and misdirected shipments.

13.5 The order will be packed as directed by the customer, if applicable.

14.0 Identification

14.1 All materials and articles will be identified by a basic part number and revision letter.

14.2 Critical materials and articles will also carry a serial or lot number. If required, a list of materials and articles by identification numbers will be attached.

12. Five Special Free Bonuses (download links are provided)

a. Excel Financial Projections Creator - simply type in your business' details and assumptions and it will automatically produce a comprehensive set of financial projections for your specific business, including: Start-Up Expenses, Projected Balance Sheet, Projected Cash Flow Statement, Financial Ratios Analysis, Projected Profit and Loss Statement, Break Even Analysis, and many more.

Copy the following link to your browser and save the file to your PC:

http://www.bizmove.com/bp/projections.xlsx

a1. Detailed guide that will walk you step by step and show you exactly how to effectively use the above Excel Financial Projections Creator.

Copy the following link to your browser and save the file to your PC:

http://www.bizmove.com/bp/projections-guide.doc

b. Simple business plan template in MS Word format - allows you to craft a good business plan quickly and easily.

Copy the following link to your browser and save the file to your PC:

http://www.bizmove.com/tools/bptemplate.docx

c. How to Improve Your Leadership and Management Skills (eBook) - Discover powerful strategies to motivate and inspire your people to bring out the best in them. Be the boss people want to give 200 percent for.

Copy the following link to your browser and save the file to your PC:

http://www.bizmove.com/bp/leadership.pdf

d. Video Training Course: How To Gain A Competitive Advantage

Learn how to get a competitive advantage with this course. Learn how to brand, study your competition, identify customers and their preferences, create pricing strategies and much more. Leverage the uniqueness of your business to create a real competitive advantage.

Copy the following link to your browser to access the online course.:

http://www.bizmove.com/business-training/how-to-gain-a-competitive-advantage.htm

e. Video Training Course: How To Grow Your Business

You have started your business and now you think you are ready to grow. How do you really know if you and your company are ready for the next step? This course will help you determine if a growth opportunity is right for you.

Copy the following link to your browser to access the online course.:

http://www.bizmove.com/business-training/how-to-grow-an-established-company.htm